EXTREME CAREERS™

BRAIN SURGEONS

Diane Bailey

rosen publishing's
rosen central®

New York

Published in 2009 by The Rosen Publishing Group, Inc.
29 East 21st Street, New York, NY 10010

Library of Congress Cataloging-in-Publication Data

Bailey, Diane.
Brain surgeons / Diane Bailey.—1st ed.
    p. cm.—(Extreme careers)
Includes bibliographical references and index.
ISBN-13: 978-1-4042-1787-4 (library binding)
1. Brain—Surgery—Juvenile literature. 2. Brain—Surgery—Vocational guidance—Juvenile literature. I. Title.
RD594.B38 2008
617.4'810233—dc22

                                                          2007042999

Manufactured in Malaysia

On the cover: Surgeons review MRI images before beginning surgery.

Contents

Introduction

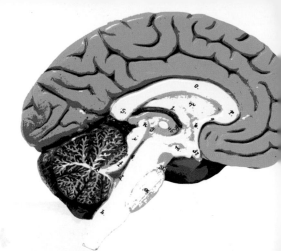

Stay out! If the brain could talk, this is probably what it would say. It was not designed for doctors to tinker with. It is wrapped in protective membranes and snugly packaged into a hard skull. The message is "Stay out!" But when the only other option is death, surgeons go in.

That's what happened one spring morning in Phoenix, Arizona, when a ten-year-old boy came into the emergency room. It's hard to surprise a doctor, but surgeons there were about to see something they'd never seen before.

The boy had been riding his bicycle when a pickup truck hit him. X-rays showed a blood clot the size of a walnut pushing against his brain stem. He had probably already suffered irreversible brain damage. Even if he hadn't, the position of the clot made it extremely difficult to reach.

But that wasn't the worst of it. As doctors looked at his X-rays, they couldn't believe what they were seeing. The boy's skull had actually been separated from his neck. The only things holding his head to his body were his spinal cord, muscles, and skin. In the realm of miracles, it was a miracle that the boy wasn't dead already.

Doctors began the surgeries needed to save the boy's life. One thing they had to do was drain the blood clot in his brain. This, by itself, was extremely risky. If the clot burst, it would bleed into his brain, which could be fatal. But they had another job: they had to reattach his skull to his spine. To do this, doctors took bone marrow from the boy's hips and put it into the vertebrae at the top of his spine, hoping it would grow into new bone.

Doctors gave the boy dismal odds. Forget about walking or talking. He was given only a 5 percent chance to survive. There were no guarantees that he wouldn't live on machines for the rest of his life.

The boy on the bike was lucky. Skill, training, and technology came together perfectly. Not only did he live, but several months later, he left the hospital. He could walk. He could talk. He could swim and climb trees. He could even ride a bike.

A Difficult Journey

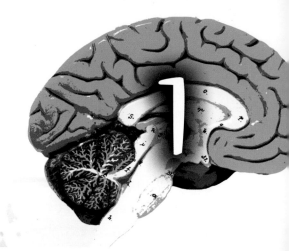

Brain surgery sounds like a "modern" career. It needs brightly lit operating rooms in clean hospitals, the latest technology, and surgeons who have trained for years. This is an accurate picture of the profession today. But brain surgery has been around for thousands of years!

Anthropologists have found ancient human skulls with holes in them. They date back to the Stone Age, about 7000 BCE. Early surgeons were in business in Africa around 3000 BCE and in Peru in 2000 BCE. Archaeologists have even found some of the tools these ancient surgeons used.

Despite the primitive conditions, these Stone Age surgeons were pretty good at what they did. In many cases, anthropologists examined the skulls and found that the bone had grown back, showing the patients lived after their surgeries.

Trephination is the practice of drilling holes in the skull. Early medicine men would make these holes in the belief that they were letting evil spirits escape. They also operated for many of the same reasons surgeons do today. For example, they tried to cure head injuries, headaches, and certain diseases like epilepsy (although they didn't know then exactly what epilepsy was).

In the Middle Ages, barbers (who knew their way around razors) were taught to be surgeons. Some unscrupulous barber-surgeons would travel around and diagnose strangely acting people by saying they had a "stone of madness" inside their heads. For a fee, the barbers would operate. They took out pieces of the "stone," which were actually pieces of brain.

But there were advancements in legitimate brain surgery, too. By the late 1800s, the first brain tumors were successfully removed. The patients

The trephination holes in this Bronze Age skull show that the wounds had started to heal. This patient survived ancient brain surgery.

frequently died soon after from infections or other complications, but they didn't die during the surgery, which was a huge step forward.

In the mid-twentieth century, another type of brain surgery caught on—the frontal lobotomy. In this operation, the frontal

7

lobe of the brain is destroyed. Since the frontal lobe controls personality and emotions, lobotomies were used to stop violent and undesirable behavior. In 1945, a man named Walter Freeman devised a truly gruesome type of lobotomy. An ice pick was inserted into the frontal lobe through a patient's eye socket and then jiggled around to destroy the connections in the brain. The "surgery" was over in a few minutes. The downside to most lobotomies was that there wasn't much of a personality left in any of the patients.

Brain surgeries used to carry extreme risk. Fifty years ago, half of them were fatal. Surgery was truly a last resort, reserved for patients who would certainly die without it. Now, the death rate has sunk to fewer than 10 percent. Also, brain surgery is often performed on patients who are not in immediate danger of dying.

The Father of Neurosurgery

Born in 1869, Harvey Cushing entered the profession of brain surgery just as it was beginning. He pioneered many techniques that later became standard, such as using X-rays to find tumors. Throughout his career, he performed more than two thousand operations, and he wrote extensively about his cases in the *Brain Tumor Registry*, which became an important reference for doctors afterward. In 1932, he formed the Harvey Cushing Society. It later became the American Association of Neurological Surgeons, which still exists today.

Cushing had many of the qualities that make up the image of the "typical" brain surgeon. He was focused, exacting, competitive, and often unforgiving of his colleagues. Walter Dandy, who also became a famous brain surgeon, was Cushing's student. However, the two clashed, and Cushing eventually dumped Dandy. They were rivals from then on.

Cushing was not perfect, of course; in those days, brain surgeries were often fatal. His assistant, Louise Eisenhardt, kept a log of

Pioneer brain surgeon Harvey Cushing works at his desk in the early 1900s. He kept records that helped future doctors.

Cushing's operations, but she wouldn't let him see it, in case he wanted to change the results in his favor.

What Is a Brain Surgeon?

Brain surgery is one aspect of the larger field of neurosurgery. Neurosurgery deals with the body's nervous system. This includes the brain, the spinal column, and nerves throughout the body. A neurosurgeon is qualified to operate on any of these areas.

Neurosurgery is divided into several subspecialties. Pediatric neurosurgeons, for example, treat children. Vascular neurosurgeons operate on blood vessels. They are sometimes called the "cowboys" of the profession because they are the ones most likely to be called in the middle of the night for emergencies like aneurysms. Other surgeons might specialize in the brain stem, where the brain connects to the spinal cord. Some surgeons will operate mostly on the spine. What ties all these together is the word "surgery." A surgeon is trained to operate. He or she deals with only those diseases or injuries that can be improved by making a physical change. However, the lines here are blurring. Problems that previously were treated by a traditional operation can now be treated with noninvasive surgeries.

Does a Brain Surgeon Have to Be a Brain Surgeon?

You've probably heard the expression, "It's not brain surgery," when whatever activity is being talked about doesn't require a lot of skill or intelligence. A brain surgeon needs to be intelligent. But you might be surprised to hear some neurosurgeons say that they don't have to be the smartest kids in the class.

At one hospital, the neurosurgeons-in-training excelled in a variety of areas. One was a pilot, another was a concert pianist, and still another was a U.S. Navy SEAL. Katrina Firlik is a brain surgeon in Connecticut. She wrote a book about her career called *Another Day in the Frontal Lobe*. In it, she describes a

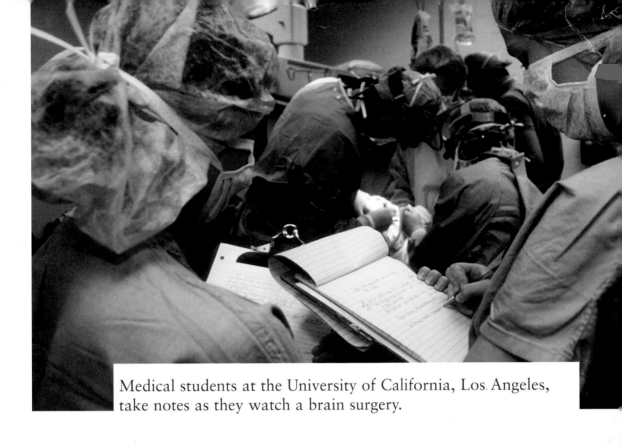

Medical students at the University of California, Los Angeles, take notes as they watch a brain surgery.

brain surgeon as part mechanic and part scientist. "Surgeons are fond of explaining that they could teach a monkey to operate," she writes. "What they mean is that operating is only part of what a surgeon does and thinks about, and it's not the hardest part."

Brain surgeons need a mix of different skills and personality traits. The words "ambitious," "authoritative," "determined," and "confident" often describe brain surgeons. They thrive looking for different solutions to a problem, and they act cool under pressure. Although they empathize with their patients, they must still keep an emotional distance.

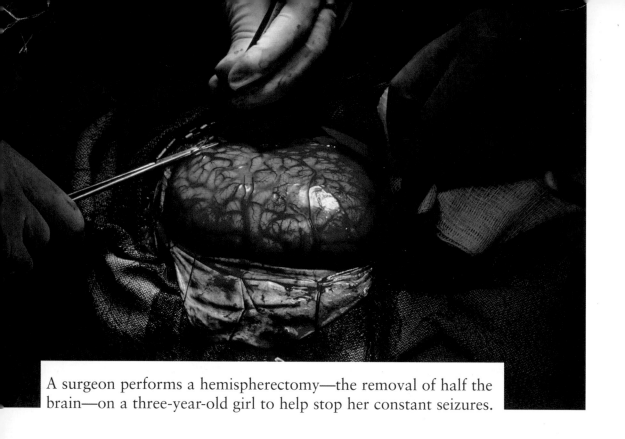

A surgeon performs a hemispherectomy—the removal of half the brain—on a three-year-old girl to help stop her constant seizures.

And it's probably a good idea not to be squeamish. One doctor was doing surgery when his patient's brain started to swell. It oozed through his fingers and started dripping onto the floor! That requires a strong stomach.

Brain surgery relies more and more on technology—and the people who are skilled with those technologies. The word "teammate" is an important part of being a brain surgeon.

Common perception is that neurosurgeons are "old"—at least in their fifties. It's true you won't see brain surgeon in their twenties. They're still in training then. But by their thirties, brain surgeons are finished with school and out working. Patients, however, may feel more comfortable with someone who's older because they think he or she will have more experience. One baby-faced neurosurgeon grew a beard so he would look older. Unfortunately, the beard made him look even younger!

An old joke goes, "The difference between God and a neurosurgeon is that God knows he isn't a neurosurgeon." Yes, brain surgeons have healthy egos. But they are aware of the huge responsibility they carry. To go into someone else's head requires the utmost confidence in one's abilities. That's not to say brain surgeons aren't impressed by the brain. They are—perhaps more so than anyone. Richard Corales, a brain surgeon from New Orleans, Louisiana, told CNN in 2000, "Your ego gets you into the specialty—and then the specialty humbles you."

Training

Becoming a doctor is a long process. After high school, there are four years of college. Then it's off to medical school, which takes another four years. (Some programs combine college and medical school into six years.) Once students complete medical school, they are technically doctors, but that doesn't mean they are ready to treat patients—at least not by themselves.

Residency begins next. The term "resident" dates to the nineteenth century, when doctors literally lived at the hospitals where they trained. They don't anymore, although many will tell you that it feels like that. Shifts can range from twelve hours to thirty-six hours. When doctors are "on" for a long time, they'll eat and sleep at the hospital, just as if they lived there.

The length of a residency depends on the doctor's specialty. Neurosurgeons and heart surgeons have the longest residencies: seven years. After that, doctors might spend another year or two in a fellowship, to further specialize. Then, they need to pass tests to get a license and become board-certified. It's no wonder there aren't that many neurosurgeons in the United States, only about 3,200.

Many years have passed by the time a neurosurgeon is ready to practice on his or her own. That eighteen-year-old high school graduate is now into his or her thirties, assuming he or she got started right away and didn't dawdle around during the past fifteen years. There is probably a mountain of debt and not much of a personal life. Still, neurosurgeons say this rigorous training is absolutely necessary. Give the job to anyone who hasn't been thoroughly prepared, and the results could be disastrous.

So why would anyone undertake this grueling existence? Well, he or she does know how to do one thing: save lives.

The Surgeon's Role

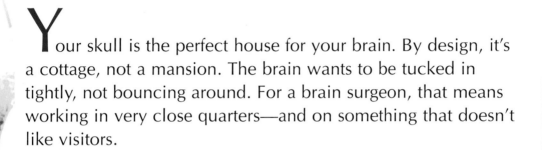

2

Your skull is the perfect house for your brain. By design, it's a cottage, not a mansion. The brain wants to be tucked in tightly, not bouncing around. For a brain surgeon, that means working in very close quarters—and on something that doesn't like visitors.

Inside the Mind

The human brain is probably the most complicated machine on earth. It makes sophisticated computers look downright clunky. It is fast, efficient, versatile, and very well built.

The brain has two halves, or hemispheres. You've probably heard the terms "right-brained" and "left-brained." The left brain controls speech and logical thinking, while the right brain handles creativity.

Each half of the brain has four lobes. The frontal lobe gets the most attention—it's where our personalities come from. The temporal lobe is responsible for hearing and memory. The

A technician works in the lab. Before surgery, a patient usually gets several tests to pinpoint the problem and help doctors choose the best treatment.

parietal lobe processes different "touch" sensations, such as pressure and pain, and the occipital lobe handles vision.

The cerebellum processes different sensory information. It's also home to the motor cortex, which directs movements. The brain stem makes sure basic life functions, such as breathing and heartbeat, are working. Of course, each part of the brain also does other things, and they work together.

The true measure of a brain isn't just the number of brain cells. "Brainpower" really comes from the connections between those cells. You'll see in pictures that the brain is wrinkly. That's so that there is more surface area, meaning there are more places to make connections. Electrical waves jump from one cell to another in order to communicate. The term "brain death" does not refer to the death of the actual cells, but to the lack of communication between them.

When Things Go Wrong

Many things can go wrong with the brain. An aneurysm, for example, is a little balloon of blood that forms in a weakened blood vessel. If it bursts, it can flood the brain with blood and kill a person instantly. Tumors, which are abnormal growths of tissue, don't threaten to end a person's life in a second. However, over time, they can grow large enough to crowd the brain and keep it from operating properly.

Traumatic brain injuries (TBI) happen when the head receives a severe blow, such as in a bicycle or car accident. They often happen because a person was not wearing a seat belt or helmet. These injuries can cause blood clots, bruising, and dangerous swelling. Swelling happens when your

The Human Brain

- Is 80 percent water, and squishy
- Weighs 3 pounds (1.4 kilograms), which is about 2 percent of an adult's weight
- Needs 20 percent of the body's fuel
- Generates the same amount of energy as a 10-watt lightbulb
- Has about 100 billion neurons, a certain type of brain cell that transmits information
- Makes trillions of connections between these neurons (Kids have twice as many connections as adults!)
- Can't feel pain
- Sends signals at the speed of up to 225 miles (362 kilometers) per hour
- Grows at the rate of 250,000 neurons per minute when a baby is in the womb

body sends more blood than usual to heal an injury. If you get a black eye or bruise your leg, there is room for the injury to swell outward. However, there is no extra space in the brain, so a person might need surgery to reduce swelling quickly and prevent death. There are many reports of surgeries done to let a person's brain swell outside the head!

One strange disease of the brain is called trigeminal neuralgia. Although the disease itself is not life-threatening, some people who suffer from it die—by suicide. It causes such intense pain in a person's face that he or she can't stand it. With other diseases, like Parkinson's disease and epilepsy, the brain's electrical signals misfire. Parkinson's patients lose their ability to control their movements. Epileptics may have convulsions, black out, or temporarily lose their ability to talk. The good news is that all of these diseases can sometimes be treated with surgery.

Lots of other diseases happen in the brain, too, such as Alzheimer's disease, autism, and depression. These cannot be helped with surgery—at least not yet.

Knowing Where to Look

In 1848, a man named Phineas Gage was working on the railroad when an iron bar blasted through his head. Amazingly, Gage survived the accident, but he was never the same. He became surly and argumentative and was unreliable at work. Eleven years later, he developed seizures, probably from his brain injury, and died.

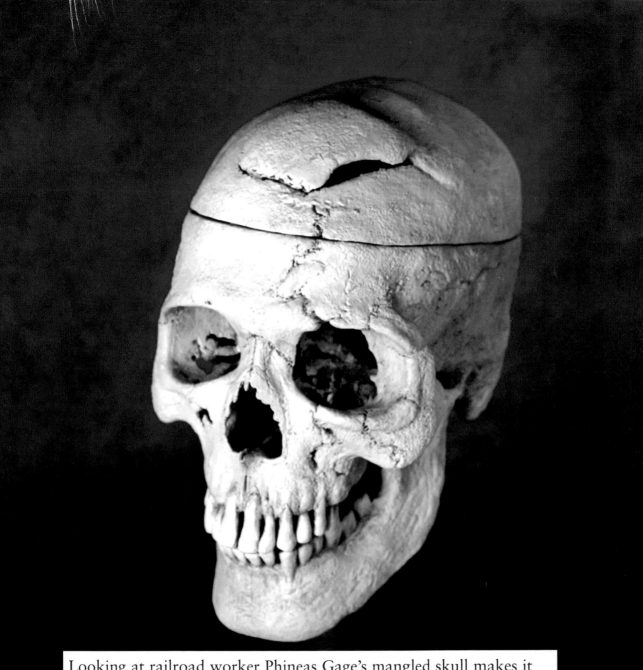

Looking at railroad worker Phineas Gage's mangled skull makes it hard to believe he survived his violent accident, but he lived for another decade afterward. His brain was severely injured, however, and his behavior changed radically.

However, Gage's case helped scientists understand that different parts of the brain control different behaviors. This is called localization. Brain surgery used to involve a lot of guesswork. Surgeons didn't know exactly where to look, so the patient went through a longer and more grueling surgery. Now, a surgeon does not have to search all through a patient's head to find the problem. He or she knows where to look.

Of course, developments in technology have also helped in the search. Before surgery, a patient gets a number of tests. A computed tomography (CAT) scan takes a lot of X-rays and combines them into a three-dimensional picture. This shows the doctor where a problem is. Magnetic resonance imaging (MRI) scans can distinguish between different kinds of tissues in the brain. A functional MRI (fMRI) actually shows brain activity.

In some brain surgeries, the doctor actually wakes up the patient during the operation. He or she asks the patient to perform several tasks, such as counting or naming pictures. At the same time, the patient is getting an fMRI to show which parts of the brain are being used to answer the questions. This way, the surgeon can be sure to steer clear of critical parts of the brain needed for speech or reasoning. A surgeon may need to tunnel through a lot of brain tissue in order to reach the source of the problem, but with a little scouting beforehand, he or she can pick the least dangerous route. This requires a great deal of precision.

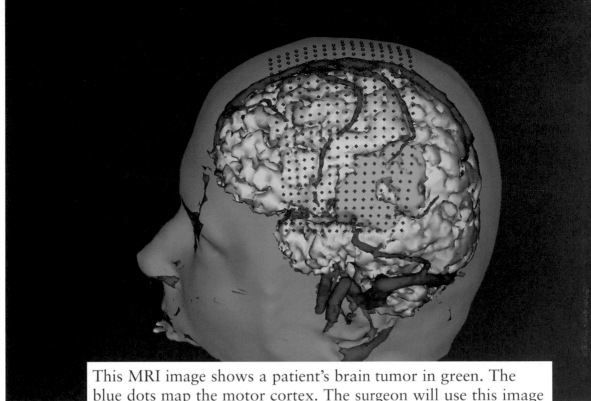

This MRI image shows a patient's brain tumor in green. The blue dots map the motor cortex. The surgeon will use this image to minimize damage to the rest of the brain when the tumor is being removed.

Going In

Brain surgeons have a lot of different operations in their repertoires. They may have to dig out a tumor. They may have to seal off (or "clip") a bloated aneurysm. They may have to remove a blood clot. A big danger during brain operations is bleeding. When sharp instruments meet the thin, fragile walls of veins and arteries, bleeding can be fast—and fatal.

Dramatic problems call for dramatic solutions, and maybe nothing is more dramatic than a hypothermic arrest. During

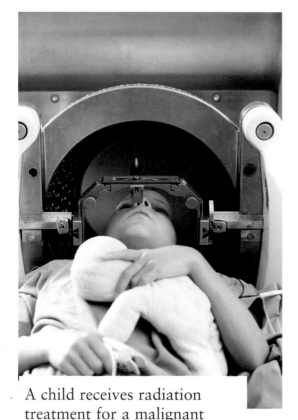

A child receives radiation treatment for a malignant brain tumor.

this rare operation, the body is cooled to far below its normal temperature, and the patient's blood is pumped out of his or her body. Normally, the brain can survive only a few minutes without fresh oxygen. However, at this low temperature, cells can make it much longer. At a body temperature of 60 degrees Fahrenheit (15.6 degrees Celsius), for example, the brain can survive an hour. The brain is essentially put "on hold," giving the surgeon time to operate. Afterward, the patient is warmed up and given back his or her blood.

Deep brain stimulation (DBS) is a technique that can help people with abnormal or disrupted brain activity, such as Parkinson's patients. In a DBS operation, the surgeon implants tiny electrodes (like computer chips) into the person's brain. These electrodes "run interference" by sending out a signal that confuses the electrical signals sent out by the brain. Although DBS does not cure Parkinson's—this disease has no cure—it can help relieve the debilitating symptoms.

Noninvasive surgeries are becoming more common. The Gamma Knife, used to kill tumors, isn't a knife at all. It's actually a couple of hundred sharp beams of radiation that are shot into a person's head from a special helmet. The radiation kills diseased tissue but misses the healthy brain around it. You could think of it as laser tag—but the playing field is much smaller. (And the target isn't trying to get away.) Some people are too fragile to withstand traditional "open-brain" surgery but can take the Gamma Knife. However, it is not effective on all types of tumors.

Difficult Decisions

Surgeons like to fix things. Sometimes, however, a problem is not fixable. New doctors will often suggest extreme measures, even though there is only a small chance they will work. Or, perhaps the surgery would solve one problem, but the patient has other life-threatening injuries. Sometimes, the best decision is to do nothing.

Operating on the brain is an incredibly delicate procedure. A surgeon may have superb technical skill, but it's more important that he or she first have the judgment to make good decisions. After all, surgery sometimes makes patients worse.

Many of the body's organs, such as the heart or lungs, are absolutely critical to survival. So is the brain. The brain not only decides if a person lives, but how that person lives. There's no wiggle room with the heart. If it works, you live. If it doesn't, you die. But with the brain, parts of it may work, while others don't. Brain injuries—and surgeries—can mean death. Or, they might cause a person to be paralyzed or in a coma.

Humans need to breathe, send blood around their bodies, and digest food. Those are the basics. But people also value what makes them unique individuals. What if you no longer liked to cook or skateboard? What if you couldn't recognize your mother? To lose your memories or personality—things your brain controls—would be devastating.

Brain surgeons must be keenly aware of these factors. They know that surgery doesn't only determine whether someone lives or dies. It could change who a person fundamentally is.

The Life of a Surgeon

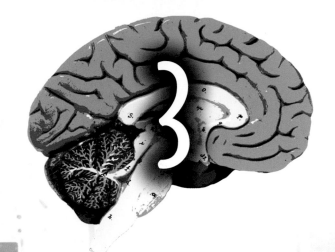

3

Question: How do you hide something from a surgeon? Answer: Give it to his family. That's a joke among surgeons, but there's quite a bit of truth in it. Unfortunately, brain surgeons don't always get to spend much time at home. Twelve-hour days are common, and sometimes they run longer.

Awake Before Dawn

Surgeons sometimes say that they get up earlier than fishermen. They may be removing a brain tumor before the sun rises, and they can't even drink coffee to help wake them up because the caffeine could make their hands shake! After surgery, it's time for morning rounds to check on their patients in the hospital.

Some of the job is just boring drudgery. There's reading, managing staff, and going to meetings—not particularly exciting stuff, but it's part of a surgeon's professional life. He or she must also consult with new patients and their families. Because brain surgery carries such a high risk, it's important that people know

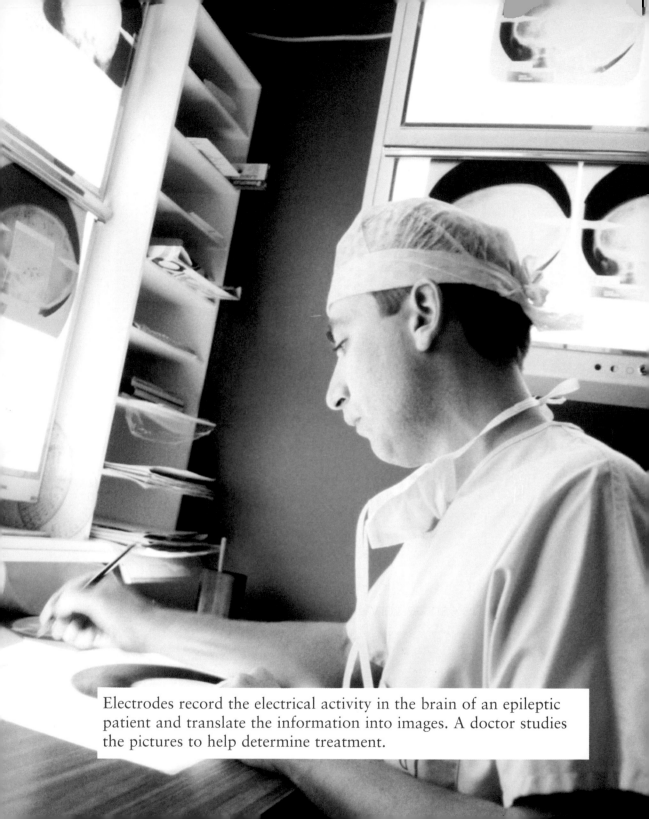

Electrodes record the electrical activity in the brain of an epileptic patient and translate the information into images. A doctor studies the pictures to help determine treatment.

what they're getting into. A surgeon must fully explain all the potential benefits and risks of a surgery. Sometimes patients don't want to hear the downside, but the surgeon has to make them listen anyway.

Surgery itself takes a lot of planning. What do surgeons dread when they go inside someone's head? Is it a tumor the size of a grapefruit? An aneurysm that's swollen and ready to burst? Actually, they've seen all that. The worst thing to see is something they didn't expect. They don't want any surprises. If they know what they're facing, they can prepare for it. They can do the necessary research, consult with other doctors, make a plan, practice the procedure in their heads, and consider possible problems.

In *The Healing Blade: A Tale of Neurosurgery*, neurosurgeon Robert Spetzler says, "You go over the procedure, and over it again, and over it again . . . On the night before a major case, of course, you never really sleep. You half-sleep. Running things through your mind."

Through the Swinging Doors

Brain surgeries can be very complex, but some of them—at least to a brain surgeon—are more common and familiar. That's not to say they are "routine." No matter how straightforward an operation is, there's no slacking when a patient is on the operating table. The surgeon has to be careful and concentrate.

Think about eating a bowl of cereal. Pretty easy, right? Now, add in a few more factors. How about eating that bowl of cereal while standing thirty feet in the air on a tree limb during a windstorm? Now, every movement—simple movements you make every day—could throw you off balance. Suddenly, there's a lot more at stake than just spilled milk. That's how it is with brain surgery.

Surgeons have different styles and preferences, too. With many procedures, there is more than one way to approach it. Which way a surgeon chooses may be dictated by the patient's individual condition. Or, the surgeon may pick the way he or she feels most comfortable. Different surgeons have different strengths. If there's a choice, each surgeon will likely decide to do what he or she is best at.

Brain surgeries are usually long. Four to eight hours is common, but several take twelve hours—and some take even longer. It takes a lot of stamina to stand up this long and to concentrate both physically and mentally. Don't surgeons need to take a break to eat or go to the bathroom? In long surgeries, yes. But because they are so focused on what they're doing, they are often able to put off these things until it's convenient.

You might think operating rooms are quiet, serious places. Actually, many surgeons play music—from classical to country. The operating staff will chat with each other. However, they avoid talking about the patient's chances, especially if those chances aren't good. Even under anesthesia, a patient may hear people talking and remember what they said. When the surgery reaches a particularly difficult point, the surgeon may ask for silence temporarily while he or she focuses. Otherwise, however, the general mood is often relaxed.

The A-Team

Operating rooms are sometimes called operating "theaters"—and every person must play his or her part flawlessly.

So who does what? Different operations will require different people, but in general, each one will have at least two surgeons: a lead surgeon and an assistant. There's also a scrub nurse who assists the surgeon by handing him or her tools and a circulating nurse whose job is to coordinate things and ensure the patient's safety by keeping an eye on him or her at all times.

This brain surgeon uses a special eyepiece to let him see tiny details.

29

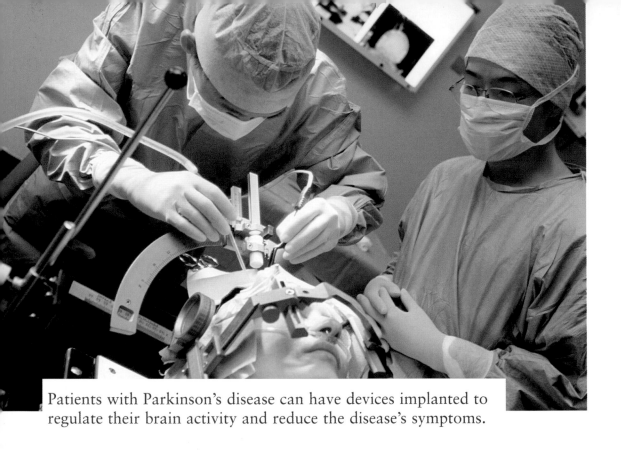

Patients with Parkinson's disease can have devices implanted to regulate their brain activity and reduce the disease's symptoms.

A key team member is the neuroanesthesiologist, who gives anesthetics to the patient. However, instead of trying to prevent pain, which is often the reason people get anesthetics, the neuroanesthesiologist's job is to reduce brain activity. Brain surgeons really don't want their patients to wake up and start squirming on the table. But they don't want them sleeping for hours afterward either. They want them to wake up so they can see how they're doing. The neuroanesthesiologist must give enough anesthetic—but not too much.

If possible, the team members are the same people every time so they are familiar with how each person works. This lets them work a little smoother and a little faster. That teamwork could save critical seconds.

Pros . . .

Given the huge responsibilities a brain surgeon faces, it might be hard to imagine why someone would choose this as a career. Indeed, many surgeons have asked themselves this same question!

The obvious answer is money. Sure, hefty salaries are a great perk. Doctors in general make good money. Surgeons make even more, and neurosurgeons are at the top of the list. In private practice, a brain surgeon could make half a million dollars a year. But it takes a long time to get there. If money is someone's goal, there are easier ways to make it.

Probably the most important answer is that a brain surgeon can save someone's life or improve his or her quality of life. When a surgeon operates on the victim of a motorcycle accident, she may give that twenty-year-old man a future. She takes patients who are dying and brings them back so that they can say "thank you."

To some people, the challenges of the job are irresistible. Brain surgeons are often people who are naturally attracted to difficult problems that need solutions. With surgery, they can find an answer to a problem and then use their own hands to put it to work.

Neurosurgeon Deon Louw said in an interview with Salary.com, "Everything that's interesting about humans, from a Brahms' symphony to weapons of mass destruction, is a function of the brain. Can you conceive of anything more fulfilling than trying to crack the code of the final frontier?"

Also, the job comes with a lot of prestige. It's pretty easy to impress people if you can say you're a brain surgeon. Brain surgeons have keen minds and unparalleled physical skills. They also have the discipline to develop these things through years of training. It's no wonder they are so respected.

... and Cons

There are significant downsides to the job, too. Unlike people in other "extreme careers," surgeons don't put their own lives in danger. Instead, they literally hold the lives of others in their hands. This responsibility creates an enormous amount of pressure when a surgeon is bent over the operating room table. In medicine, it's not the effort that counts. It's the result. A surgeon must strive to produce good results, sometimes under nearly impossible circumstances.

Of course, sometimes patients die. This is a part of any surgeon's life, but especially brain surgeons. The surgeon must learn how to prepare a patient and his or her family for this risk. If it happens, he must break the bad news. The surgeon must also deal with the death himself. All surgeons must learn how to emotionally separate themselves from their patients. If a surgeon is devastated by a patient's death, he will not make an effective doctor. He must be able to move on to the next patient. This

Brain surgeons sometimes have to deliver bad news. Here, a surgeon fields questions at a press conference about a girl, born with two heads, who died after surgery.

does not mean that a surgeon cannot learn from a patient's death. Doctors attend regular "morbidity and mortality" (M&M) meetings to discuss such things.

Sometimes doctors are held responsible when a surgery has a negative outcome. Neurosurgeons carry insurance to protect them if a patient or his or her family sues for malpractice. Malpractice means the surgeon did not do everything he was supposed to in order to prevent a bad result. Legal actions like these are not uncommon. Patients or their families may win millions of dollars. For this reason, malpractice insurance is extremely expensive.

Brain surgeons make a lot of personal sacrifices, too. Emergencies have a way of happening at inconvenient times. The surgeon may get called during her son's soccer game or in the middle of the night. If she's the one on call, then she can forget about cheering on her son or getting a good night's sleep. A patient's life comes first.

Triumphs and Tragedies

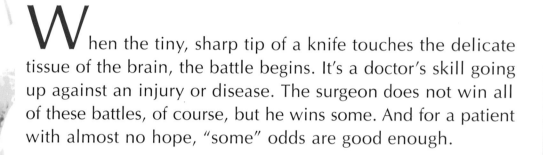

4

When the tiny, sharp tip of a knife touches the delicate tissue of the brain, the battle begins. It's a doctor's skill going up against an injury or disease. The surgeon does not win all of these battles, of course, but he wins some. And for a patient with almost no hope, "some" odds are good enough.

Separating the Twins

In 1987, Dr. Benjamin Carson, a pediatric neurosurgeon, performed an extraordinary surgery. Two German boys had been born as conjoined twins, also known as Siamese twins. Their bodies were connected to each other at the backs of their heads. It's very risky to separate conjoined twins because they are connected on the inside, too. Their circulatory systems may be tied together, and they may share organs, such as a liver. Their bodies may rebel if these are disturbed.

When the parents of the German twins looked into the possibility of surgery, one doctor told them that there was

Twin girls, just under a year old, are joined at the head. Surgery to separate conjoined twins is complicated and risky, but the success rate is growing.

no way to save the lives of both boys. One of them—at least—would most likely die.

However, Dr. Carson thought he could do the surgery. The parents decided to take the risk. For five months, Dr. Carson planned the operation. He practiced, using dolls, in several "dress rehearsals." The real operation took twenty-two hours and required a team of seventy doctors, nurses, and other staff. There were many tense moments as the twins endured massive bleeding. But in the end, they both made it. They were the first twins ever to survive such a surgery.

Talking Without Words

People who have had strokes or who have certain brain diseases can lose their ability to speak. Imagine how frustrating this must be, especially for people who still have all their mental abilities. They know exactly what is going on. They know what they want to say. They simply can't say it.

In 1998, at Emory University in Atlanta, Georgia, surgeons found a solution for one man who had suffered a stroke. They implanted a special computer chip into his brain. The chip picked up the electrical signals in his brain and sent them to a computer. The power generated by his brain signals could move a cursor on a screen. The man then learned to control the electrical signals in his brain so he could control the cursor. His thoughts acted like a computer mouse. He moved the cursor around to icons on the screen, and the computer then spoke different phrases. His favorite? "See you later. Nice talking with you."

Boosting Brainpower

In 2007, doctors inserted electrodes into the brain of a thirty-eight-year-old man. He had been in a "minimally conscious state" for six years after a severe brain injury. This is not as severe as a coma. However, although the man occasionally showed signs of awareness, he could not function normally.

For example, he might blink or move his fingers, but he couldn't talk or use his arms enough to feed himself.

Doctors knew that the man's brain still worked to some degree. What they wanted to do was give his brain function a boost. Doctors believed that by producing more electrical signals in the man's brain, they would give his own brain cells a jolt of energy. It would rev up their activity enough so that other parts of his brain could respond to them.

The surgery was done in two parts and took ten hours. Afterward, the man started to use words and gestures, and he was able to answer questions. He was also able to chew and swallow food, so he didn't need a feeding tube anymore. His mother said the man had gotten back a quality of life that they never thought he would have.

Small Miracles

Most brain surgeries do not have the breakthrough results as the ones just described. But to a patient who gets a life he thought he would never have, they are small miracles.

Take the case of a woman who had been diagnosed with Alzheimer's disease. Among other things, Alzheimer's causes patients to lose touch with reality. The woman was living in a nursing home. She came in with a large, but benign, brain tumor. A neurosurgeon spoke with the woman's family and found that she had been functioning well until the last couple of years.

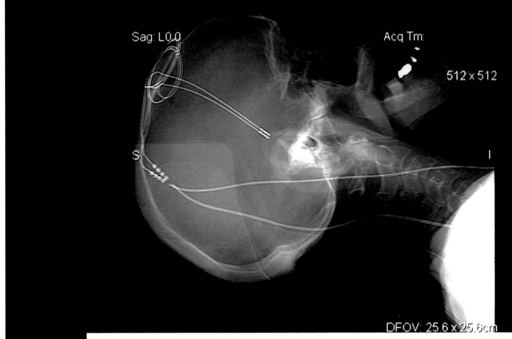

An X-ray shows electrodes that stretch from the surface of the skull deep into the brain. Deep brain stimulation (DBS) can help control brain activity in Parkinson's patients.

Maybe she didn't have Alzheimer's. The surgeon decided there was a possibility—maybe slight, but a possibility—that the tumor was affecting her brain, and removing it could give her back her mental functions. He was correct. After the surgery, the woman recovered fully. She left the nursing home and went back to her life.

Benjamin Carson, the pediatric neurosurgeon, has performed many hemispherectomies. In this drastic and complex operation, one entire half of the patient's brain is removed. People who have seizure disorders, such as epilepsy, can benefit from this

A doctor displays the right side of a three-year-old girl's brain, which was removed to help stop her intense seizures. The left side of her brain took over the functions of the right side.

surgery. In a healthy brain, each side takes care of different functions. But people who have lost arms or legs often learn to do things another way. The brain also has a remarkable ability to adapt.

Dr. Carson operated on one little girl and removed the left half of her brain, which controls speech. After the surgery, her parents walked beside her as she was being wheeled down the hallway to the recovery room. The girl opened her eyes, saw her parents, and said, "I love you." Although the "speech" center of her brain was gone, the rest of it had found a way.

Another of his patients suffered severe bleeding during an operation to remove a tumor. She made it through the operation, but she was essentially brain-dead. Doctors were almost certain there was no way she could get better. However, after a few days, she moved a finger. Months later, she left the hospital. Scientifically, it's impossible to explain how people can recover like this. But these stories tell about the awesome power of the brain, and how surgeons must respect it.

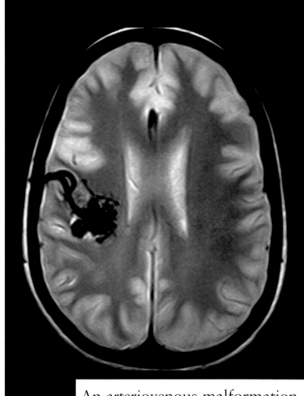

An arteriovenous malformation (AVM) is obvious on this MRI image. AVMs can be extremely difficult to remove.

Losses

Death is an inescapable part of the brain surgeon's world. Many times, an injury is simply too severe. No surgery can help. Other times, surgery might help, but the patient isn't strong enough to survive the trauma of an operation.

Think of a rubber-band ball. That's kind of what an arteriovenous malformation (AVM) looks like. It's essentially a ball of tangled up blood vessels. Removing an AVM is tedious and dangerous because a patient needs some of the vessels, but

Speed Surgery

Explosions, vehicle accidents, gunshot wounds—these are all daily occurrences in war. During World War I, traumatic brain injury (TBI) gave neurosurgery some of its first patients. Now, TBI has been called the "signature injury" of the war in Iraq. More than two thousand soldiers have been diagnosed with some form of TBI, and there may be thousands more.

At an air force hospital in Balad, Iraq, getting surgery is much different from surgery in a regular hospital. Fortunately, for the injured soldiers, the medical facilities there are equipped to handle major surgeries fast. One soldier was rushed in, had tests run, and was on the operating table in less than twenty minutes! Also, surgeries that can take several hours in a traditional hospital stateside might be done in half an hour.

One man with a severe brain injury

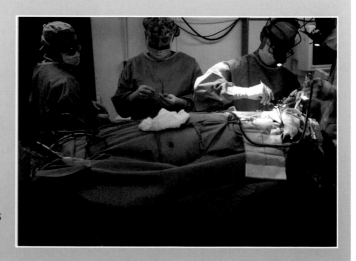

Brain surgeons operate on an Iraqi man at the Balad Air Force Theater Hospital in Iraq, where both Americans and Iraqis receive treatment.

was given only a 1 percent chance of survival. But he also had some of the best surgeons in the world working on him. "I cried, I prayed, I cussed, and I screamed," his wife told *Discover* magazine. "After a few days, [my husband] turned his head toward me and said, 'Enough already. I'm going to be OK.'"

not all of them. Like defusing a bomb, the surgeon must be careful not to snip the wrong cord.

In her book *Another Day in the Frontal Lobe*, neurosurgeon Katrina Firlik writes about the case of one young woman who underwent surgery to remove an AVM. She survived the actual surgery. However, after a few hours, her brain began to bleed. The AVM had been part of her brain for years. Her circulatory system was used to it. Her brain could not tolerate the change, and she died.

Sometimes, of course, mistakes are made during an operation, and sometimes patients die because of them. There are different types of mistakes. The worst is a mistake made because someone was careless or negligent. Other times, even with planning, things just go wrong. For example, aneurysms are usually taken care of by "clipping." The surgeon attaches a clip to the blood vessel, cutting off blood flow to the aneurysm. However, aneurysms can be extremely delicate. The tiniest wrong movement can cause the aneurysm to burst. This does not mean that the surgeon is unskilled, or that he or she was negligent in any way. It only means that sometimes things go wrong. Surgery is not a perfect science, and the body is not a perfect machine.

The Future of Brain Surgery

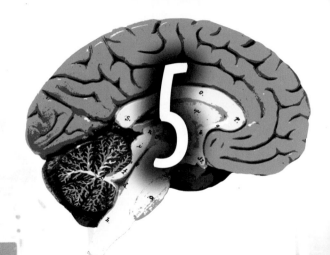

In 1989, President George H. W. Bush proclaimed the 1990s the "decade of the brain." During those ten years, scientists learned a lot about how the brain functioned and how to fix it when it didn't function. Although the decade of the brain has passed, the learning—and the possibilities—have not.

A New Frontier

Although surgeons have eagle eyes and steady hands, the terrain of the brain is small. A good surgeon might be able to work within a field that's an eighth of an inch (.32 centimeters) across. Microscopes and magnifying lenses help, but sometimes surgery requires an even smaller view.

In 2007, at the University of Calgary in Canada, researchers announced a new machine called NeuroArm. This robotic tool can fit in a space that's only as wide as a hair. A surgeon controls the arm from a computer. The machine is designed to feel the same way it would if a surgeon was actually holding the

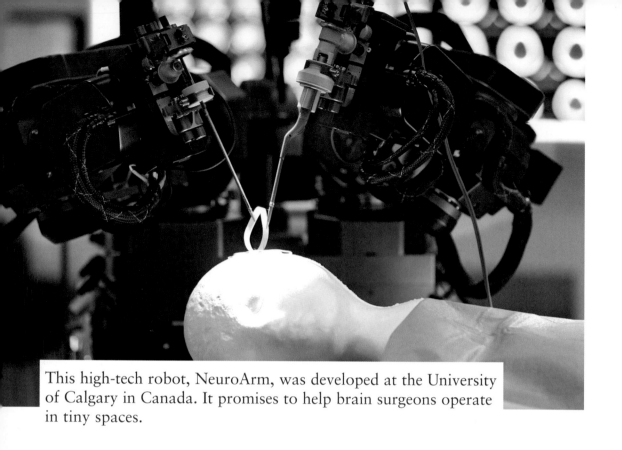

This high-tech robot, NeuroArm, was developed at the University of Calgary in Canada. It promises to help brain surgeons operate in tiny spaces.

instruments. A new operating room called BrainSUITE was recently opened at a hospital in Houston, Texas. Inside, cameras on the ceilings show magnified pictures of the brain. Huge "data billboards" display information on vital signs. There's also an extra-large MRI scanner, so if the surgeon wants to check his work, he simply swivels the operating table inside it.

Different types of surgery are also being introduced. Deep brain stimulation (DBS) already can help Parkinson's patients. Now, scientists hope that it might be used for other diseases, like epilepsy, depression, and eating disorders.

Some operations involve putting new tissue into the brain. This tissue may come from other parts of the patient's body or from stem cells. Even brain transplants may be on the horizon. In fact, this has already been done, in 1970—but the patient was a monkey, not a human. In the operation, the entire head of one animal was transferred to another. The monkey survived the surgery and lived for another week.

Not all brain surgeries require going through the head. In endonasal surgery, doctors get to the brain through a patient's nose. Certain patients may not get surgery because of their religious beliefs. Jehovah's Witnesses, for example, do not believe in blood transfusions (receiving someone else's blood). This is often necessary during traditional surgeries. Endonasal surgery can sometimes give the surgeon a way around this problem.

Controlling the Mind

People get face-lifts to look better. What if you could think better? "Brain-lifts" may be in the future. Electrodes can stimulate brain activity. Conceivably, they could be used to improve anything from memory to musical performance. Maybe that idea seems strange, but just over a century ago, most people would have thought a face-lift was bizarre. Although brain-lifts are still a product of the future, they are close enough that the scenario is not entirely science fiction.

The idea comes with a whole set of problems. There are physical risks, as with any surgery, but the bigger issues are ethical ones. Many people object to the idea of meddling with the mind, especially if there is nothing actually wrong. Also, insurance companies probably would not pay for these operations. Only people with money could afford them—and they would not come cheaply. Some people worry that they could create a bigger gap between rich people and the rest of society. Wealthy people could become smarter and more accomplished, and everyone else would still be—everyone else.

And what about children? Parents usually make major decisions concerning their children's health. Should they have the right to choose such a surgery for their children? Or would that violate a person's right to choose for him- or herself?

You've probably heard about drugs called steroids. Evidence shows that athletes who use steroids can improve their physical performance. The drugs build up their muscles, so the athletes get stronger and faster. Most sports leagues do not allow using steroids. Steriod use is considered an unfair advantage because steroids are not a natural way, such as training, to beef up the body.

The idea of surgery to improve the brain is even more thorny. With steroids, a person decides by himself whether he will take them. In a surgery, at least two people are involved—the patient who will benefit and the surgeon who performs the operation. This makes it an ethical question for both parties involved. Not surprisingly, "neuroethics" is a big topic of discussion.

Actor Christopher Reeve supported stem cell research that might lead to treatments for people with severe spinal injuries, such as the one he suffered after a horse-riding accident. Reeve died in 2004.

Other Controversies

You might hear about cutting-edge surgeries in the news. But these developments didn't happen overnight—they just got publicized overnight. First, there were years of research and experiments.

Stem cell research plays a large role in finding new ways to treat brain diseases and injuries. Stem cells are brand-new cells that have not yet turned into a particular type, such as a brain cell, a blood cell, or a skin cell. They are pieces of biological clay that the body shapes into what it needs.

Scientists can collect these stem cells before they develop. Then, they can direct them to grow into a particular kind of cell. Stem cell research is extremely controversial. Some people think it's a case of scientists "playing God"—messing around where they don't belong. Also, most stem cells come from embryos—babies still growing in the womb. Some people fear that stem cell research could lead to women trying to sell their developing babies to researchers who want the stem cells.

Scientists usually experiment on animals before trying something on humans. Animal rights activists frequently oppose using animals for this purpose. For one thing, they believe it is inhumane. They also argue that it might not even be effective. After all, something that works on a rat, a dog, or a monkey may not work on a human.

Even when something will technically work, there are other things for the surgeon to consider. Take the case of a brain transplant. Would it be right to give a person a brain that didn't come with his or her body? What if one was a boy and the other was a girl? The body and the brain are supposed to be a matching set, not "sold separately."

Also, putting electrodes into a person's brain to control behavior could have serious consequences. It's one thing to help a paralyzed person gain control of his or her arms and legs. But what if scientists started directing people, like robots? It's almost like something out of a science fiction film.

At the Flick of a Switch

In the 1960s, a scientist named José Delgado put an electrode into a bull's brain. He could operate the electrode with a remote control. Then, Delgado got in a ring with the bull, which charged him. A matador can distract a bull with a flick of a red cape. Delgado had no cape, but he had his remote. A split second before the bull reached him, Delgado flicked the switch on the remote. Instantly the bull stopped and turned away. Delgado had put the electrode into the part of the brain that controlled aggression. By pushing the button, he short-circuited the animal's natural tendency to charge. Delgado suggested electrodes could be used in certain people, such as violent criminals. However, the scientific community balked at the idea.

Delgado's bull had an on/off switch, but what about rats with steering wheels? Recently, scientists implanted electrodes into rats' brains. They stimulated pleasure centers in the animals' brains to direct their movements. They "taught" them to turn right or left, and took advantage of their natural abilities to learn new behaviors, such as how to climb a tree. Scientists hoped the rats could be used to sniff out land mines or to find people in disaster areas.

Keeping an Open Mind

Will the brain surgeon ever go out of style? The job itself, probably not. But the types of people who do it may change. The profession relies more on technology and teamwork than it used to. The image of the individual at the top of the field—skilled, independent, perhaps even arrogant—may not accurately describe future brain surgeons.

Operating on a brain aneurysm used to require traditional surgery. Now, the same condition may be treated by putting a catheter (a thin tube) into the patient's leg and threading it up to the aneurysm. Then, small coils are fired through the catheter, sealing off the aneurysm so it doesn't pop. This procedure, called embolization, does not require a surgeon. A radiologist can do it. However, some surgeons are not delegating the job. They are getting the additional training they need to do the procedure.

Neurosurgeon Robert Spetzler said in *The Healing Blade: A Tale of Neurosurgery*, "It is not an unglorious occupation to put yourself out of business. That requires all of the very best talents. The sin is to try to hang on to the past only to have a profession, rather than using discoveries to make a glorious step into the future, to be part of whatever comes next."

Trim, snip, shape: the job of a neurosurgeon will change in little ways with each new development. Open-brain surgery may become less common. But even if the head stays closed, those who try to heal it will have to keep an open mind.

Glossary

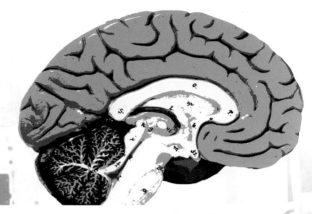

Alzheimer's disease A disease that causes a person to lose his or her mental abilities, resulting in behavior changes and memory loss.

anesthetic A drug given to reduce pain and brain activity during surgery.

aneurysm A bubble of blood that forms on a blood vessel.

electrode A small chip that conducts electricity.

empathize To understand what another person is feeling.

epilepsy A brain disorder that causes seizures.

hemispherectomy The removal of one hemisphere, or half, of a person's brain.

hypothermic arrest Cooling a person's body temperature in order to temporarily stop the body's function.

lobotomy The destruction of a lobe of the brain or separating its connections to the rest of the brain (usually refers to the frontal lobe).

malpractice When a doctor does not do what he or she is professionally obligated to do, resulting in a negative outcome for the patient.

neuroethics The study of ethical issues related to brain science.

neuron A type of brain cell that is responsible for communicating with other cells.

noninvasive surgery A type of surgery that does not require physically entering the head.

Parkinson's disease A brain disease that causes people to lose control of their movements.

seizure A misfiring of the brain's electrical signals, sometimes resulting in loss of motor control, speech, or mental faculties.

stem cell A cell that can develop into any type of cell.

steroids Technically called anabolic steroids. Drugs that cause the body's cells to produce more protein and develop muscle; used to enhance physical performance.

stroke A rapid loss of brain function because the brain is not getting enough blood.

traumatic brain injury A sudden and severe brain injury, usually caused by a physical blow.

trephination The practice of drilling holes in the skull.

tumor An abnormal growth of tissue.

vascular Having to do with blood vessels.

For More Information

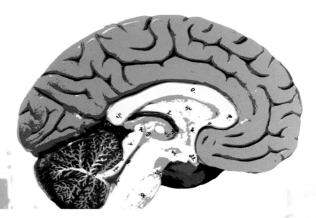

American Association of Neurological Surgeons
5550 Meadowbrook Drive
Rolling Meadows, IL 60008
(847) 378-0500 or (888) 566-AANS (2267)
E-mail: info@aans.org
Web site: http://www.aans.org
The AANS offers professional support to surgeons and
    information about neurological surgery to the public.

Brain Injury Association of America
1608 Spring Hill Road, Suite 110
Vienna, VA 22182
(703) 761-0750 or (800) 444-6443
E-mail: info@biausa.org
Web site: http://www.biausa.org
The Brain Injury Association of America promotes awareness
    of traumatic brain injuries and helps people who have
    been affected by them.

Congress of Neurological Surgeons
10 North Martingale Road, Suite 190
Schaumburg, IL 60173
(847) 240-2500 or (877) 517-1CNS (1267)
E-mail: info@1CNS.org
Web site: http://www.neurosurgeon.org
The Congress of Neurological Surgeons promotes education
and scientific research devoted to neurosurgery.

National Institute of Neurological Disorders and Stroke (NINDS)
NIH Neurological Institute
P.O. Box 5801
Bethesda, MD 20824
(301) 496-5751 or (800) 352-9424
Web site: http://www.ninds.nih.gov
NINDS directs and funds research related to neurological
diseases.

The Neurological Sciences Federation
Canadian Neurosurgical Society
7015 Macleod Trail SW, Suite 709
Calgary, AB T2H 2K6
Canada
(403) 229-9544

E-mail: info@cnsfederation.org

Web site: http://www.ccns.org

The Canadian Neurosurgical Society is a Canadian professional organization promoting the knowledge and practice of neurosurgery.

Web Sites

Due to the changing nature of Internet links, Rosen Publishing has developed an online list of Web sites related to the subject of this book. This site is updated regularly. Please use this link to access the list:

http://www.rosenlinks.com/exc/brsu

For Further Reading

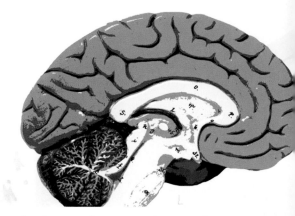

Carson, Ben, with Cecil Murphey. *Gifted Hands*. Grand Rapids, MI: Zondervan Publishing House, 1990.

Fleischman, John. *Phineas Gage: A Gruesome but True Story About Brain Science*. Boston, MA: Houghton Mifflin Company, 2002.

Goldsmith, Connie. *Neurological Disorders*. Woodbridge, CT: Blackbirch Press, Inc., 2001.

Landau, Elaine. *Head and Brain Injuries*. Berkeley Heights, NJ: Enslow Publishers, Inc., 2002.

Newquist, H. P. *The Great Brain Book*. New York, NY: Scholastic Inc., 2004.

Woods, Michael, and Mary B. Woods. *Ancient Medicine: From Sorcery to Surgery*. Minneapolis, MN: Runestone Press, 2000.

Bibliography

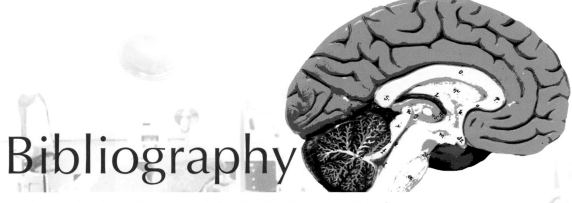

Arkins, Audrey. "Dream Job: Brain Surgeon." Salary.com.
Retrieved August 1, 2007 (http://www.salary.com/careers/
layouthtmls/crel_display_Cat10_Ser131_Par231.html).

Bard, Arthur, and Mitchell Bard. *The Complete Idiot's Guide
to Understanding the Brain.* Indianapolis, IN: Pearson
Education, Inc., 2002.

Chelvarajah, Ramesh. "Brain Surgery . . . Not Rocket Science."
BMJ Careers, Vol. 328, No. 7439, March 6, 2004, pp. 95–96.

Emory University Health Sciences Center. "Emory
Neuroscientists Use Computer Chip to Help Speech-
Impaired Patients Communicate." *ScienceDaily*,
November 11, 1998. Retrieved September 7, 2007
(http://www.sciencedaily.com/releases/1998/11/
981111080706.htm).

Firlik, Katrina S. *Another Day in the Frontal Lobe: A Brain
Surgeon Exposes Life on the Inside.* New York, NY:
Random House, Inc., 2006.

Hopkin, Michael. "Implant Boosts Activity in Injured Brain."
Nature, Vol. 448, No. 7153, August 2, 2007, p. 522.

Jost-Vu, Elke. "Deep Brain Stimulation: Desert Spine and Neurosurgical Institute Offers New Treatment." Eisenhower Medical Center. *Healthy Living*, June–August 2007. Retrieved August 1, 2007 (http://www.emc.org/body.cfm?xyzpdqabc=0&id=489&action=detail&ref=281).

Mason, Michael. "Dead Men Walking." *Discover*, March 2007, pp. 54–62.

Miller, Craig A. *The Making of a Surgeon in the 21st Century*. Nevada City, CA: Blue Dolphin Publishing, Inc., 2004.

Noonan, David J. *Neuro: Life on the Frontlines of Brain Surgery and Neurological Medicine*. New York, NY: Simon and Schuster, 1989.

Oglesby, Christy. "Brain Work Requires Endurance, Ego." CNN.com, December 4, 2000. Retrieved August 1, 2007 (http://www.cnn.com/fyi/interactive/news/brain/brain.surgeon.html).

Petaschnick, JoAnn. "Brain Mapping Provides Direction for Surgeons." Medical College of Wisconsin. HealthLink, January 27, 2006. Retrieved August 1, 2007 (http://healthlink.mcw.edu/article/1031002587.html).

Rainer, J. Kenyon. *First Do No Harm*. New York, NY: Villard Books, 1987.

Salter, Chuck. "This Is Brain Surgery." *Fast Company*, January 1998, p. 146.

Smith, Carol. "Inside the World of the Brain Surgeon." *Seattle Post-Intelligencer*, January 18, 2002. Retrieved August 1, 2007 (http://seattlepi.nwsource.com/local/54988).

Sylvester, Edward J. "The Boy Who Beat the Odds." *Ladies' Home Journal*, January 1990, pp. 94–95, 157–158.

Sylvester, Edward J. *The Healing Blade: A Tale of Neurosurgery.* New York, NY: Simon and Schuster, 1993.

University of Calgary. "World's First Image-Guided Surgical Robot to Enhance Accuracy and Safety of Brain Surgery." *ScienceDaily*, April 19, 2007. Retrieved August 1, 2007 (http://www.sciencedaily.com/releases/2007/04/070417114732.htm).

University of Pittsburgh Medical Center. "A New Approach to Brain Surgery." *UPMC HealthJournal.* Retrieved August 1, 2007 (http://healthjournal.upmc.com/0405/Endonasal Surg.htm).

Vertosick, Frank T. *When the Air Hits Your Brain: Tales of Neurosurgery.* New York, NY: W.W. Norton & Company, Inc., 1996.

Index

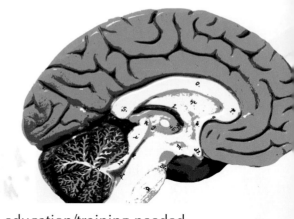

About the Author

While preparing this book, Diane Bailey was fascinated to learn about how brains function. She has a lot of respect for surgeons who have devoted their entire lives to earning the right to touch them. Bailey has two children and writes on a variety of nonfiction topics.

Photo Credits

Cover, pp. 22, 26, 30 © Phanie/Photo Researchers, Inc.; p. 1 and additional page backgrounds © www.istockphotos.com/ Baloncici; pp. 4, 6, 15, 25, 35, 45, 53, 55, 58, 59, 62 © www. istockphotos.com/Doctor_bass; p. 7 © SSPL/The Image Works; p. 9 © Hulton Archive/Getty Images; p. 11 © Lara Jo Regan/ Liaison/Getty Images; pp. 12, 40 © Joe McNally/Getty Images; p. 16 Shutterstock.com; p. 19 © The Image Works; p. 21 © MIT AI Lab/Surg., Planning Lab, BWH/Photo Researchers. Inc.; p. 29 © Roger Ressmeyer/Corbis; p. 33 © Juan Barreto/AFP/Getty Images; p. 36 © UCLA/Getty Images; pp. 39, 41 © Living Art Enterprises, LLC/Photo Researchers, Inc.; p. 42 © Chris Hondros/Getty Images; p. 46 © AP Images; p. 49 © Alex Wong/Getty Images.

Designer: Les Kanturek **Editor:** Bethany Bryan
Photo Researcher: Cindy Reiman